ARABIC FOR YOU

Fifth Edition
Fourth Edition

SOLAYMAN KABOOH

رقم الإيداع ٥٤ / ١٥ / ٩٧

الترقيم الدولى .I.S.B.N

977 - 19 - 5075 - 4

- First Edition 1997 by the author.

- Second Edition 1999 by the author.

- Third Edition 2000 by the author.

- Fourth Edition 2002 by the author.

- **Fifth Edition 2004 by the author.**

Contents

Chapter Three : Conversation

Chapter One

Arabic Alphabet

Alif	A	As in Cāt	١	Used as a vowel
Alif Mahmouzah or Hamzah	A'	As in Aback	أ	or ء
	E' or I'	As in England / India	إ	or ء
	U'	as in Ukraine	أ	or ء
Bā'	B	As in Book	ب	(ـب) (ـبـ)
Tā'	T	As in Talk	ت	(ـت) (ـة)
Thā'	Th	As in Think	ث	(ـث) (ـثـ)
Jeem	J	As in Jam	ج	(ـجـ)
'Hā'	'H	It has no English equivalent	ح	(ـحـ)
Khā'	Kh	It has no English equivalent	خ	(ـخـ)
Dāl	D	As in Door	د	(ـد)

Thāl	Th	As in This	ذ	(ـذ)
Rā'	R	As in Rabbit	ر	(ـر)
Zay	Z	As in Zero	ز	(ـز)
Seen	S	As in Say	س	(ـس)
Sheen	Sh	As in Show)	ش	(ـشـ)
Ṣād	Ṣ	(as in Salt)	ص	(ـصـ)
Dhad	Dh	It has no English equivalent	ض	(ـضـ)
Ṭā'	Ṭ	It has no English equivalent	ط	(ـطـ)
Żā'	Ż	It has no English equivalent	ظ	(ـظـ)
'Ayn	'A	It has no English equivalent	عَ	(عَـ)
				(ـخَ)
	'I or 'e	It has no English equivalent	عِ	(عِـ)
				(ـحِ)
	'O or 'U	It has no English equivalent	عُ	(عُـ)
				(ـحُ)

10

Ghayn	Gh	It has no English equivalent	غ	(غـ) (ـغـ)
Fā'	F	As in Fat	ف	(فـ) (ـفـ)
Qāf	Q	It has no English equivalent	ق	(قـ) (ـق)
Kāf	k	As in Keep	ك	(كـ) (ـكـ) (ـك)
Lām	L	As in Loss	ل	(لـ) (ـلـ) (ـل)
Meem	M	As in Man	م	(مـ) (ـمـ)
Noon	N	As in Noon	ن	(نـ) (ـنـ) (ـن)
Hā'	H	As in Hand	هـ	(هـ) (ـهـ)
Wāw	W	As in Well	و	(ـو)
Yā'	Y	As in Yes	ى	(يـ) (ـيـ)

Remarks

- Alif Mahmouzah is a variant form of the letter Alif which is governed by the context of speech.
- For the purpose of this book, in case the letter ع ('Ayn) is followed by the vowel Alif Mad (ا) it will be indicated by this character : ('ā)
- For the purpose of this book, in case the vowel Alif Mad (ا) is followed by Hamzah (ء) it will be written like this (Ā')
- Words in brackets are Egyptian dialects.
- Listen to the tape to know how the sound 'Ha (ح) is pronounced. Some of the Arabic words which contain this sound are indicated here under

Sweet = (Helw) حلو   Red = (a'Hmar) أحـمر

Donkey = (Himār) حمار   Lawyer = (Mu'Hāmei) محـامى

Horse = 'HiṢān حصان   Dates = (Bala'H) بـلح

- Listen to the tape to know how the sound 'Ayn (ع) is pronounced. Some of the Arabic words which contain this sound are indicated here under

Returned = ('Āda) عاد   Teacher = (Mu-'alim) معـلـم

Worked = ('Amila) عمل

Rubbed = (D'aka) دعــك

Scientist = ('Ālim) عالم Heard = (Sami-'a) سمع

- The Arabic sound Dhād (ض) is nearly pronounced like (d) in Doll and mud. Some of the Arabic words which contain this sound are indicated here under

    Hit = (Dharaba) ضرب Officer = (DhābiṬ) ضابط

- Listen to the tape to know how the Arabic sounds Ṭā' (ط) and Ẓā' (ظ) . are pronounced. Some of the Arabic words which contain the sound Ṭā' (ط) are indicated here under

    Potato = (BaṬāṬah) بطاطة = (Ṭabei-'ah) طبيعة

    Student = (Ṭālib طالب Melon = (BaṬeikh) بطيخ

- As for the sound Ẓā' (ظ) , following are some of the Arabic words which contain it

    Appeared = (Ẓahara) ظهرَ Dark = (Ẓalām) ظلام

13

- You should differentiate between the Arabic sounds Tā' (ت) and Ṭā (ط). The first is voiceless and the second is voiced. The tape will help you to pronounce them correctly.
- You should also differentiate between the Arabic sounds Dāl (د) and Dhād (ض). The first is voiceless (as in the word Mohammed) and the second is voiced (as in the word Doll and Mud. The tape will help you to pronounce them correctly.

- There is a difference in pronunciation between the sounds Thāl (ذ), Zay (ز), and Ẓā'(ظ). The first is pronounced as in "This", the second as in "Zero", while the third has no English equivalent and the tape will help you to pronounce correctly.

Ex. for Ẓā' (ظ) words like : Appeared = (ẓahara) ظَهَرَ,

Dark = (ẓalām) ظلام

- Likewise, there is a difference in pronunciation between the sounds Seen (س) and Thā'(ث). The first is

14

pronounced as in "Summer", and the second as in "Thought".

- There is also a difference between Seen (س) and Şad
(ص) . The first is voiceless (as in "Since" and the second is voiced and in pronunciation it is nearer to the word "Salt".

الحَرَكات وحـروف المَـد

Al-'Harkāt wa 'Huroof Al-Mad

Arabic Vowels

There are six Arabic vowels; three of them are short vowels and are called in Arabic "Al-'Harkāt", and the other three are long and called in Arabic "Huroof Al-Mad" The short vowel (Al-'Harkāt) are :

1. Al-Fat-'Hah. Its phonetic symbol is "   " . It is indicated in writing by a sloping stroke over the letter. In this book it will be represented by "ä" or "a"

* Examples : حَضَـرَ which is pronouced ('Hadhara) and means (He came) .

2. Al-Kasrah. Its phonetic symbol "   " . It is indicated in writing by a sloping stroke below the letter. In this book it will be represented by either "i" or "e".

* Example : كِتـاب .which is pronounced (kitāb) and means (Book) . The letter (كِ) here has a kasrah under it, so we pronounce it (ki).

3. <u>Al-Dhammah</u>.   Its phonetic symbol is " ´ " . It is
indicated in writing by a small (wāw) on the letter. In
this book it will be represented by "u" or "o".

● Example : مُدَرِسة which is pronounced (Mudarresah) and

means (a woman teacher) . The letter (م) here has a

dhammah over it, so we pronounce it (mu) .

<u>The long vowels (Huroof Al-Mad) are :</u>
1. <u>Alif Mad :</u> When "al-fat-'Hah" is extended it becomes
"alif mad" and is indicated in writing by the letter "١"

without "hamzah" (ء). In this book it will be represented

by "ā"
● <u>Example :</u>
    Door   Bāb   باب

2 . <u>Yā' Mad</u>   : If al-kasrah is extended it becomes "Yā'
Mad" and is represented by the letter "ي", and for the
purpose of this book it will be represented by the characters
"ei" as in Beat , Nosebleed

* Example :
  Honest Amein   أمــيــن

3. Wāw Mad : When al-dhammah is extended it becomes "wāw mad", and is indicated in writing by the letter waw (و). For the purpose of this book it will be represented by the English vowel "oo" like "bone"
* Example :
  Market Sooq   ســوق

* * *

Notes.
* The absence of the three vowels on the letter means skoon (silence). It is indicated with the mark " ° " on the letter
* Changing the vowel's position may change the meaning of the word, For instance the word مُدَرسة (female teacher) if we changed the vowel Dhammah into Fat-'Hah it becomes مَدْرسة (madrasah) which means school.

- It is not necessary in this book to know when to change vowels.
- In case of Alif Mahmoozah (E', I' or U') it may be written at the beginning of words in this way (E, I, or U)

Examples

أمثلة

Alif	A	ا
كتاب	شباك	باب
Kitāb	Shibbāk	Bāb
Book	Window	Door
Alif Mahmuzah	**A'**	**أ (ء)**
أكرم	أمان	أحمد
Akram .	Amān	A'Hmad
(Proper Noun)	Security	(Proper Noun)
Alif Mahmuzah	**I'**	**إ**
إقامة	اسماعيل	إكرامى
Iqāmah	Ismā-'eil	Ikrāmei
Setting up	(Proper Noun)	(Proper Noun)
Bā'	**B**	**ب**
بــيت	بــطاطس	بــلح
Bayt	BaṬāṬis	Bala'H
Home	Potatoes	Dates

ت	T	Tā'
تكتب	تنام	تدرس
Taktub She writes	Tanām She sleeps	Tadrus She studies
ث	Th (as in think)	Th
ثــروت	ثــورة	ثــروة
Tharwat (Proper Noun)	Thawrah Revolution	Tharwah Wealth
ج (ــحـ)	J	Jeem
جــيد	جـــميل	جـــو
Jayyid Good	Jameil Beautiful	Jaw Atmosphere
ح (ــحـ)	H	Hā'
حــمار	حِــلْو	حــضرَ
'Himār Donkey	'Helw Sweet	'Hadhara He came
خ (ــخـ)	Kh	Khā'
خــبير	خـــادم	خـــمسة

21

Khamsah Five	Khādem Servant	Khabir Expert
Dāl	D	د (ــد)
دراجة	دولة	دم
Darrājah Bicycle	Dawlah State	Dam Blood
Thal	Th (as in this)	ذ (ــذ)
يـذاكر	ذهب	ذكى
Yuthākir He studies	Thahab Gold	Thaki Intelegent
Rā'	R	ر (ــر)
رمسيس	رمضان	رجب
Ramsis Ramsis	Ramadhān Ramadan (Arabic Month)	Rajab Rajab (Arabic Month)
Zay	Z	ز (ــز)
زميل	زمن	زينب
Zameil Fellow	Zaman Time	Zaynab (Proper Noun)

<u>Seen</u>	<u>S</u>	س (ـس)
سائح	سـعيد	سـمك
Sāi''H Tourist	Sa-'eid Happy	Samak Fish
Sheen	Sh	ش (ـش)
خـرشـوف	مـشـمـش	الـشـمس
Kharshoof Antishoke	Mishmish Apricots	Al-shams The Sun
Şad	Ş (as in Salt)	ص (ـص)
صـدر	يـصـدر	صناعة
Şadr Chest	YuŞaddir He exports	Şinā'ah Industry
Dhad	Dh	ض (ـض)
ضـرر	ضـرورى	ضـابط
Dharar Harm	Dharoori Necessary	DhābiŢ Officer

Ṭā'	Ṭ	ط (ـط)
طبخ	طالب	طابع
Ṭabkh	Ṭālib	Ṭābi-'e
Cooking	Student	Stamp
Ża'	Ż	ظ (ـظ)
ظرف	ينـظر	ظـهـرَ
Żarf	Yanżur	żahara
Envelope	He looks	He appeared
'Ayn	'A	ع (ـعـ) (ـعـ)
		(ـع)
عـادَ	عـمـلَ	عـادل
'Aāda	'Amila	'Aādil
He returned	He worked	Just
Ghayn	Gh	غ (ـغـ) (ـغـ)
		(ـغ)
غـرب	غـدا	غـائب
Gharb	Ghadan	Ghāi'b
West	Tomorrow	Absent
Fā'	F	ف (ف) (ـف)

يفـكر Yufakkir He thinks	فـوق Fawq Above	فـاهم Fāhim Understanding
Qāf	Q	ق (قـ) (ـق)
قـال Qāl He said	قـمر Qamar Moon	يـقـتل Yaqtulu He kills
Kāf	K	ك (ـكـ) (ـك)
كـراسة Kurrāsah Notebook	كـلام Kalām Speech	كـبير Kabeir Big
Lām	L	ل (ـلـ)
لـيل Layl Night	لـبن Laban Milk	لـحمة La'Hmah Meat
Meem	M	م (ـمـ)
مـلابس Malābis Clothes	مـال Māl Money	مـطر MaṬar Rain
Noon	N	ن (ـن) (ـنـ)

نـظيف	نـاجح	نـاعم
Naẓeif Clean	Nājih successful	Nā-'im Smooth
هـ (ـهـ)(ـه)	H	Hā'
هـرب	هـجم	هـجرة
Haraba He escaped	Hajama He attacked	Hijrah immigration
و (ـو)	W	Wāw
ولد	وطن	وادى
walad Boy	WaTan Homeland	Wādi Valley
ى (يـ)(ـيـ)	Y	Yā'
يـزود	يـجرى	يـلعب
Yuzawwid He provides	Yajri He runs	Yal'ab He plays

Chapter Two

General Words

Family Members

Father	Ab	أب
Mother	Um	أم
Brother	Akh	أخ
Sister	Ukht	أخت
Son	Ibn	ابن
Daughter	Ibnah	ابنة
Grandfather	Jad	جد
Grandmother	Jaddah	جدة
Husband	Zawj	زوج
Wife	Zawjah	زوجة
Uncle (paternal)	'Am	عم
Uncle (maternal)	Khāl	خال
Aunt (paternal)	'Ammah	عمة
Aunt (maternal)	Khālah	خالة

Marriage	Zwāj	زواج
Death	Mawt	موت
Life	'Hayāh	حياة

* * *

Positions

King	Malik	ملك
Queen	Malikah	ملكة
President	Ra'eis	رئيس
Consul	QunŞul	قنصل
Minister	Wazir	وزير
Judge	Qādhy	قاضى
Writer	Kātib	كاتب
Editor	Mu'Harrir	محرر
Engineer	Muhandis	مهندس
Physician	Ţabeib	طبيب
Teller	Şarrāf	صراف

Accountant	Mu'Hāsib	محاسب
Author	Mua'llif	مؤلف
Inspector	Mufattish	مفتش
Headmaster	Nāżir	ناظر
Teacher	Mudarris	مدرس
Officer	DhābiŢ	ضابط
Lawyer	Mu'Hāmy	محامى
Manager	Mudeir	مدير
Policeman	ShurŢy	شرطى
Employee	Muważaf	موظف
Nurse	Mumarredhah	ممرضة
Undertaker	'Hānuty	حانوتى

* * *

Crafts

| Carpenter | Najjār | نجار |

Electrician	Kahrabā'iy	كهربائى
Jeweler	Jawahirjy	جواهرجى
Watchmaker	Sā'āti	ساعاتى
Ironer	Makwajy	مكوجى
Hairdresser	Hallāq	حلاق
Tailor	Tarzy	ترزى
Dressmaker	Tarzy Hareimy	ترزى حريمى
Grocer	Baqqāl	بقال
Greengrocer	Khudhary	خضرى
Shoemaker	Jazmajy	جزمجى
Plumber	Sabbāk	سباك
Labourer	'Āmil	عامل
Guard, Watchman	Ghafeir	غفير
Doorkeeper	Bawwāb	بواب
Butcher	Jazzār	جزار

Places

Capital	'ĀṢimah	عاصمة
Ministry	Wizārah	وزارة
Town, City	Madeinah	مدينة
Village	Qaryah	قرية
Harbor, Port	Meinā'	ميناء
Airport	MaṬār	مطار
Station	Ma'HaṬah	محطة
Square	Maydān	ميدان
Bridge	Kubry	كوبرى
School	Madrasah	مدرسة
Hospital	Mustashfa	مستشفى
Pharmacy	Ṣaydaliyyah	صيدلية
Clinic	'Iyādah	عيادة
Theatre	Masra'H	مسرح
Embassy	Sifārah	سفارة

33

Consulate	QunȘuliyyah	قنصلية
Hotel	Funduq	فندق
Factory	MaȘn'a	مصنع
Company	Sharikah	شركة
Office	Maktab	مكتب
House	Manzil	منزل
Flat	Shaqqah	شقة
Building	Mabna	مبنى
Street	Shāri-'e	شارع
Garden	'Hadeiqah	حديقة
Museum	Mut-'Haf	متحف
College	Kulliyah	كلية
Customs Office	Jumruk	جمرك
Room	Ghurfah	غرفة
Shop	Dukkān	دكان
Library	Maktabah	مكتبة
Book shop	Maktabah Tujāriyyah	مكتبة تجارية

English	Transliteration	العربية
Market	Sooq	سوق
Restaurant	MaŢ'am	مطعم

* * *

Meals

English	Transliteration	العربية
Breakfast	IfŢār	إفطار
Dinner	Ghadā'	غداء
Supper	'Ashā'	عشاء
Jam	Murabba	مربى
Honey	'Assal	عسل
Milk	Laban	لبن
Cheese	Jibn	جبن
Sweet	'Halāwah	حلاوة
Meat	La'Hmah	لحمة
Liver	Kibdah	كبدة
Kidney	Kalāwi	كلاوى

Pigeon	Ḥamām	حمام
Chicken	Dajāj	دجاج
Goose	Wiz	وز
Duck	BaṬ	بط
Turkey	Rumy	رومى
Potatoes	BaṬāṬis	بطاطس
Peas	Bisillah	بسلة
Okra	Bāmyah	بامية
Spinach	Sabānikh	سبانخ
Squash	Koosah	كوسة
Mlukia	Mulookhiyah	ملوخية
Macaroni	Makaroonah	مكرونة
Rice	Urz	أرز
Cucumber	Khiyār	خيار
Lettuce	Khas	خس
Onions	BaṢal	بصل
Salad	SalaṬah	سلطة

Sauce	ŞalŞah	صلصة
Pepper	Filfil	فلفل
Oil	Zeit	زيت
Butter	Zibdah	زبدة
Tomatoes	ȚamāȚim	طماطم
Bread	'Eish - Khubz	عيش – خبز
Salt	MalʿH	ملح
Fruits	Fākihah	فاكهة
Vegetables	Khudhrāwāt	خضراوات
Cabbage	Kurunb	كرنب
Carrots	Jazar	جزر
Mangoes	Mangah	مانجه
Banana	Mooz	موز
Orange	Burtuqāl	برتقال
Apples	TuffāʿH	تفاح
Dates	BalaʿH	بلح
Grapes	'Inab	عنب

Melon	Shammām	شمام
Watermelon	BaTeikh	بطيخ
Peach	Khawkh	خوخ
Juice	'ASir	عصير
Coffee	Qahwah	قهوة
Tea	Shāy	شاى
Sugar	Sukkar	سكر
Beer	Birah	بيرة
Cold Drink	Mashroob Bārid	مشروب بارد

* * *

Utensils

Fork	Shawkah	شوكة
Spoon	Mal'aqah	ملعقة
Knife	Sikkein	سكين
Plate	Ṭabaq - ṢïHn	طبق – صحن

Pan	Ṭāsah	طاسة
Pot	Qidr - 'Hallah	قدر – حلة
Cup	Finjāl	فنجال
Glass	Koob	كوب
Refrigerator	Thallājah	ثلاجة
Waiter	Jarsoon	جرسون
Cook	Ṭabbākh	طباخ
Dining Table	Sufrah	سفرة

* * *

Furniture

Bedroom	'Hujrat Al-Noom	حجرة النوم
Sitting Room	'Hujrat Al-Juloos - Al—Ṣaloon	حجرة الجلوس - الصالون
Living Room	'Hujrat Al-Ma-'eishah	حجرة المعيشة
Office	Maktab	غرفة المكتب

Kitchen	MaṬbakh	مطبخ
Bath	Hammām	حمام
Hall	Ṣālah	صالة
Entrance	Madkhal	مدخل
Bed	Sireir	سرير
Carpet	Sajjādah	سجادة
Pillow	Mikhaddah	مخدة
Mattress	Martabah	مرتبة
Chair	Kursy	كرسى
Table	Mindhadah	منضدة

* * *

Colours

Black	Aswad	أسود
Blue	Azraq	أزرق
Brown	Bunni	بنى

Green	Akhdhar	أخضر
Emerald	Akhdhar zumurrudy	أخضر زمردى
Red	A'Hmar	أحمر
Scarlet	A'Hmar ghāmiq	أحمر غامق
Gray	Ramādi	رمادى
Orange	Burtuqāli	برتقالى
Beige	Beij	بيج
Cream	kreim	كريم
Golden	Thahaby	ذهبى
Pink	Wardy	وردى
Purple	Banafsejy	بنفسجى
Silver	Fadhy	فضى
White	Abyadh	أبيض
Yellow	AŞfar	أصفر

Post Office

Post Office	Maktab Al-Bareid	مكتب البريد
Telephone Office	Maktab Al-Telefoonāt	مكتب التليفونات
Letter	KhiṬāb	خطاب
Stamp	Ṭābi-'e	طابع
Parcel	Ṭard	طرد
Card	Kārt	كارت

*   *   *

Directions

Right	Yamein	يمين
Left	Yasār	يسار
Outside	Khārij	خارج
Inside	Dākhil	داخل
Behind	Khalf	خلف
In front of	Amām	أمام

| Here | Hunā | هنا |
| There | Hunāk | هناك |

Garments

Blouse	Bloozah	بلوزة
Dress	Roob	روب
Shirt	QameiŞ	قميص
Skirt	Junillah	جونلة
Suit	Badlah	بدلة
Trousers	BanṬaloon	بنطلون
Coat	BalṬoo	بالطو
Hat	BarneiṬah	برنيطة
Hand Bag	ShanṬah	شنطة
Belt	'Hizām	حزام
Shoes	'Hithā'	حذاء

* * *

Adjectives

Strong	Qawy	قوى
Weak	Dha-'iyf	ضعيف
Nice, Gentle	LaṬeif	لطيف
Beautiful	Jameil	جميل
Heavy	Thaqeil	ثقيل
Light	Khafeif	خفيف
Thin	Rafe-'i	رفيع
Thick	Sameik	سميك
Broad, Wide	'Areidh	عريض
Narrow	Dhayyiq	ضيق
Tall, Long	Ṭaweil	طويل
Short	QaȘeir	قصير
Generous	Kareim	كريم
Miser	Bakheil	بخيل

Lazy	Kaslān	كسلان
Diligent	Mujtahid	مجتهد
Honest	Amein	أمين
Dishonest	Khāi'n	خائن
Mad	Majnoon	مجنون
Wise	'Āqil	عاقل
Polite	Mua'ddab	مؤدب
Clever	Māhir	ماهر
Active	NasheiṬ	نشيط
Noisy	Muz'ij	مزعج
Calm	Hādi'	هادئ
Big	Kabeir	كبير
Small	Ṣagheir	صغير

Chapter Three

Conversation

Greetings

- Welcome	Mar'Haba	مرحبا
- Good morning	ŞabāʿH al-khayr	صباح الخير
- Good morning	ŞabāʿH al-noor	صباح النور
- Good evening	Masā' al-khayr	مساء الخير
- Good evening	Masā' al-noor	مساء النور
- Good night	TiŞbaʿH 'ala khayr	تصبح على خير
- Good night	Wa anta min ahluh	وانت من أهله
- Good afternoon	Ṇāharak sa-'eid	نـــهارك سعيد
- Good bye	Ila al-liqā'	إلى اللقاء
- See you later	Arāka fima ba-'ad	أراك فيما بعد
- Peace be upon you	Al-salāmu 'alaykum	السلام عليكم
- Peace be upon you	'alaykum al-salām	عليكم السلام

Invitation

English	Transliteration	العربية
- Could you please help me?	Hal tusā-'iduni min fadhlik?	هـــل تســاعدنى مـــن فضلك؟
- I am lost. Can you show me the way	Anā tāi'h. Hal turshiduny	أنا تائه هل ترشدنى ؟
- Are you waiting for someone	Hal tantaźirein a'Hadan ?	هل تنتظرين أحدا ؟
- Can you come for dinner tomorrow night ?	Hal Yumkin an ta'ti lil ghadā' masā' al-ghad ?	هل يمكن أن تأتى للغداء مساء الغد ؟
- Can you join us for drink this evening ?	Hal tushārikunā mashruban masā' al-yum?	هل تشاركنا مشروبــــا مساء اليوم ؟
- Can I get you a drink ?	Hal Uqaddim laka mashruban ?	هل أقدم لك مشروبا ؟
- Are you free this evening ?	Hal anta fādhi al-yum?	هل أنت فاض اليوم ؟
- Would you like to go out with me ?	Hal tu'Hibbina al-khrooja ma-'iy?	هل تحبين الخروج معى ؟
- Have you got a light, please ?	Mumkin twal'a li min fadhlik ?	ممكن تولع لى من فضلك ؟
- Shall we go to the cinema ?	Hal nath-hab ila al-cinema ?	هل نذهب آلي السينما؟

- Where shall we meet ?	Ayna nataqābal ?	أين نتقابل ؟
- When shall I pick you up ?	Mata amur 'alik ?	متى أمر عليك ؟
- May I take you home ?	Mumkin awaṢalak al-manzil ?	ممكن أوصلك المنزل ؟
- Can I see you tomorrow ?	Hal araka ghadan?	هل أراك غدا ؟
- It has been a wonderful evening.	Laqad kanat sahrah mumti-'ah.	لقد كانت سهرة ممتعة .
- I have enjoyed myself.	Laqad Istamt'atu bihā.	لقد استمتعت بها .
- Do you live alone?	Hal ta-'eish waʼHdak?	هل تعيش وحدك ؟
- Do you live with your family ?	Hal ta-'eish ma'a ausratik ?	هل تعيش مع أسرتك ؟
- May I introduce my friend ?	Uqaddim laka Ṣadiqy.	أقدم لك صديقى .
- Glad to know you.	Tasharrafnā.	تشرفنا .
- How long have you been here ?	Munth mata wa anta hunā ?	منذ متى وأنت هنا ؟
- Is this your first visit ?	Hal Hathihi awwal zeyārah lak ?	هل هذه أول زيارة لك؟

- No, I have come here last year .	Lā, atitu hunā al-sanah al-mādhiyah.	لا ، أتيت هنا السنة الماضية.
- Are you enjoying your stay?	Hal anta mabsooŢ hunā?	هل أنت مبسوط هنا ؟
- Are you alone ?	Hal anta wa'Hdak?	هل أنت وحدك ؟
Where do you live ?	Ayna taskun ?	أين تسكن ؟
- What are you studying ?	Māthā Tadrus ?	ماذا تدرس ؟
- What kind of business are you in?	Māthā tashtaghil ?	ماذا تشتغل ؟

At The Cinema / Theatre

- What is on at the cinema tonight ?
Māthā fi al-cinema al-yum ?
ماذا فى السينما اليوم ؟

- What play tonight?
Ay masraʿHiyyah al-laylah?
أى مسرحية الليلة ؟

- Can you recommend me a good film ?
Mumkin tanṢaʿHuni bifilm kuwayyis ?
ممكن تنصحـــنى بفيلـــم كويس؟

- What time does it begin ?
Mata yabdaʿ ?
متى يبدأ ؟

- What time does the show end ?
Mata yantahi al-ʾardh ?
متى ينتهى العرض ؟

- Are there any tickets tonight ?
Hal tujad tathākir al-laylah ?
هل توجد تذاكر الليلة؟

- I want to reserve two tickets.
Urid an aʿHjez tathkaratayn
أريد أن أحجز تذكرتين

- I want a seat in the stalls
Urid makānan fi al-Ṣālah
أريد مكانا فى الصالة

- Where is the Opera House ?
Ayna dār al-opera?
أين دار الأوبرا ؟

- Who is singing?
Män yughanni ?
من يغنى ؟

- Who is dancing ?
Män yarquṢ ?
من يرقص ؟

- What time does the program start ?
Mata yabdaʿ al-birnāmij ?
متى يبدأ البرنامج ؟

- What orchestra is playing ?
Mā hiya al-firqah allati tʿazif ?
ما هـــى الفرقـــة الـــتى تعزف؟

- What are they playing ?	Māthā y'azifoon ?	ماذا يعزفون ؟
- Is there a floor show ?	Hal yujad 'ardh fanni?	هل يوجد عرض فنى ؟
- Are there belly dancers ?	Hal tujad raqiȘāt sharqiyyāt ?	هل توجـــد راقصـــات شرقيات؟
- Would you like to dance ?	Hal tarquȘ ?	هل ترقص ؟

* * *

At The Airport

- This is my passport	Hāthā huwa jawāzi.	هذا هو جوازى .
- I will be staying a few days.	Sawfa abqa bidh'at ayyām .	سوف أبقى بضعة أيام .
- I don`t know yet.	Lā a-'arif b`ad.	لا أعرف بعد .
- I am here on holiday .	Anā hunā fi ajāzah.	أنا هنا فى إجازة .
- I am here on business.	Anā hunā fi shughl.	أنا هنا فى شغل .
- Where is the Customs office	Ayna maktab al-jumruk	أين مكتب الجمرك .
- Give me my passport.	A-`aŢini jawāz safari.	أعطنى جواز سفرى .
- I have nothing	Laysa m`ai shaye`.	ليس معى شئ .
- Must I pay on this?	Hal yajib än adfa`a lihāthā ?	هل يجب أن أدفع لهذا ؟
- It's for my personal use.	Innaha list`emāli al-shakhŞy.	إنها لاستعمالى الشخصى
- It is not new. Can I leave ?	Innahā must`amalah. Mumkin Amshi ?	إنها مستعملة . ممكن أمشى؟

* * *

55

At the Hair Stylist's

- I want a hair cut please.	Urid qaŞ sh'ari min fadhlik.	أريد قص شعرى مـــن فضلك
I'd like a shave.	Urid 'Halq thaqni.	أريد حلق ذقنى .
- Don't cut it too short.	Lā tuqaŞirhu jeddan.	لآ تقصره جدا .
- Just a trim please.	QuŞ basiŢ min fadhlik.	قص بسيط من فضلك .
- A little more off.	QaŞar akthar min hāthā.	قصر أكثر من هذا .
- I don't want any oil.	Lā urid zeit.	لا أريد زيت .
- Would you please trim my beard	Urid tawdheib thaqni min fadhlik.	أريد توضيب ذقنى مـــن فضلك .
- How much do I owe you ?	Kam al-'Hisāb ?	كم الحساب ؟
- I'd like it cut and shape.	Urid qaŞ wa tasrei'H.	أريد قص وتسريح .
- A re-style.	Tasrei'Hah jadeidah.	تسريحة جديدة .
Colour rinse.	Ghaseil billoon.	غسيل باللون

- Shampoo and set	Shamboo wa tasreiH.	. شامبو وتسريح
- Face pack.	Shad al-wajh.	. شد الوجه
- Razor blades.	Amwās 'Helāqah.	. أمواس حلاقة
- Shaving brush.	furshit 'Helāqah.	. فرشة حلاقة
- Shaving cream.	Kreim 'Helāqah.	. كريم حلاقة
- Shaving soap.	Ṣabaoon 'Helāqah.	. صابون حلاقة
- Talcum powder.	Boudrit talk.	. بودرة تلك
- Comb.	MishṬ sha-'ar.	. مشط شعر
Colouring.	Ṣabghah.	. صبغة
Towel.	Foo'Ṭit wajh.	. فوطة وجه

* * *

Sport

- Where is the nearest sporting club ?	Ayna aqrab nādi riyādhi ?	أين أقرب نادى رياضى؟
- Where is the nearest golf courts ?	Ayna aqrab mal'ab golf ?	أيــن أقــرب ملعــب جولف؟
- Where are the tennis courts ?	Ayna malā-'ib al-tenis ?	أين ملاعب التنس ؟
- Can I hire rackets?	Hal yumkin ta'jir al-madhārib ?	هــل يمكــن تأجـــير المضارب؟
- Is there a swimming pool ?	Hal yujad 'Hammām sibā'Hah?	هل يوجد حمام سباحة ؟
- Can we swim in the lake ?	Hal yumkin än nasta'Him fi al-bu'Hayrah ?	هل يمكن أن نستحم فى البحيرة ؟
- I'd like to see boxing match .	Urid mushāhadat mubārāt mulākamah .	أريد مشــاهدة مبــاراة ملاكمة .
- Can you get me two tickets ?	Hal yumkin shirā' tathkaratayn ?	هــل يمكــن شـــراء تذكرتين؟

- Is there a football match ?	Hal tujad mubārāt kurat qadam ?	هل توجد مباراة كـــرة قدم ؟
- Who is playing ?	Män yal'ab ?	من يلعب ؟
- Where is the beach?	Ayna al-shāṬei'	أين الشاطئ
- Is it safe for swimming ?	Hal al-istiʾHmām āmin ?	هل الاستحمام آمن ؟
- Is it safe for children	Hal huwa amān lil aṬfāl ?	هل هو أمان للأطفال ؟
- It's very calm.	Innahu hādei' jiddan	إنه **هادئ** جدا
- Are there dangerous currents?	Hal tujad tayyarāt khaṬirah ?	هل توجد تيارات خطيرة ؟
- Where can I buy a bathing suit from ?	Min ayna ashtari māyooh ?	من أين أشتري مايوه .؟
- Is there a bathing hut ?	Hal tujad kabeinah likhal'a al-malābis?	هل توجد كابينة لخلـــع الملابس ؟
- A swimming belt.	ʾHizām najāh	حزام نجاة
- A motor boat.	Lansh	لنش
- A rowing boat.	Markib bimagādeif.	مركب بمجاديف
- A sailing boat.	Markib sherā-'ei.	مركب شراعى

59

- What is the charge for one hour ?	Bikam al-sā'ah ?	بكم الساعة ؟
- I want to hire . . .	Urid Isti'jār . . .	أريد استئجار . . .
- Is there a youth hostel ?	Hal yujad beit lil shabāb ?	هل يوجد بيت للشباب؟
- Is there a camping site ?	Hal yujad mu-'askar?	هل يوجد معسكر ؟

* * *

Emergency

- Can you get me a doctor ?	UTlub li doctor min fadhlik.	اطلب لى دكتــور مـــن فضلك
- When will he come?	Mata ya'ti	متى يأتى ؟
- Here is an accident.	Yujad Hādith	يوجد حادث .
- Is any one hurt ?	Hal USeib aHad ?	هل أصيب أحد ؟
- It's all right, don't worry.	Lā taqlaq, al-umoor Tabiy'iyyah.	لا تقلق ، الأمور طبيعية
- Where is the nearest hospital ?	Ayna aqrab mustashfa	أين أقرب مستشفى ؟
- Call the nurse.	UTlub al-mumarridhah	اطلب الممرضة .
- Can you mind acting ?	Hal yumkin an tash-had	هل يمكن أن تشهد ؟
- Call the police.	UTlub al-boleis	اطلب البوليس .
- Call the ambulance.	UTlub al-is'āf	اطلب الإسعاف .
- He is dying.	Innahu yamoot	إنه يموت .

- He is not taking a breath.	Innahu lā yatanaffas	إنه لا يتنفس .
- Stop that man.	Imsik hāthā al-rajul	امسك هذا الرجل
- Stop, thief.	Imsik, 'Harāmi	امسك ، حرامى
- Come here.	Ta-' āla hunā	تعال هنا .
- Stop here.	Qif hunā	قف هنا .
- It's fire.	Innahu 'Hareiq	إنه حريق .
- It's dangerous	Innahu kha'Teir	إنه خطير .
- Come in quickly.	Udkhul bi sur'ah	ادخل بسرعة .
- Go away at once.	Insarif fi al-'Hāl	انصرف فى الحال .
- Lie down now.	Urqud al-ān	ارقد الآن .
- Call the electric office.	U'Tlub maktab al-kahrabā'	اطلب مكتب الكهرباء .
- Call the electrician.	U'Tlub al-kahrbāi'y	اطلب الكهربائى .
- Please help me.	Arjook, sā-'idni	أرجوك ساعدنى .
- Where is nearest phone ?	Ayna aqrab telefoon?	أين أقرب تليفون .

* * *

Shopping

- How much is this?	Bikam hāthihi ?	بكم هذه ؟
- I don't pay more than . . .	Anā lā adfa-'a akthar min . . .	أنا لا أدفع أكثر من . .
- I will take it.	Sa-ākhuth-hā	سآخذها .
- Can I have a receipt ?	Mumkin fātoorah ?	ممكن فاتورة ؟
- Do you accept dollars ?	Hal taqbal dolārāt ?	هل تقبل دولارات ؟
- Can I pay a traveler's cheque ?	Mumkin adfa-'a shik?	ممكن أدفع شيك ؟
- Haven't you made a mistake ?	Alaysa hunāk khaṬa'?	أليس هناك خطأ ؟
- I want to return this.	Urid irjā-'a hāthihi.	أريد إرجاع هذه .
- I'd like a refund.	Urid istirdād al-thaman.	أريد استرداد الثمن .
We don't accept.	Hāthā marfoodh.	هذا مرفوض .
- Where is the nearest place to . . .?	Ayna aqrab makān ila . . . ?	أين أقرب مكان الى . . ؟
- Where do they sell.. ?	Ayna yubā-'a . . . ?	أين يباع . . . ؟

- How can I get there ?	Kayfa aṢil ilayh ?	كيف أصل إليه ؟
- Have you . . . ?	Hal 'indak . . . ?	هل عندك . . . ؟
- Can you help me ?	Hal yumkinuka musā-'adati ?	هل يمكنك مساعدتى ؟
- Where can I find . . . ?	Ayna ajidu . . . ?	أين أجد . . . ؟
- Can you order it for me ?	Hal yumkinuk an tooṢi 'alayhā ?	هل يمكنك أن توصى عليها؟
- How long will it take ?	Mata takoon jāhizah?	متى تكون جاهزة ؟
- Please send it to this address.	Min fadhlik arsilhā 'ala hāthā al-'inwān.	من فضلك أرسلها على هذا العنوان.
- Can you measure me. . . ?	Hal taqeis li . . . ?	هل تقيس لى . . . ؟
- I don't know your sizes.	Anā lā a-'arif maqāsātikum.	أنا لا أعرف مقاساتكم
- Can I try this on ?	Hal yumkin an aqeis hāthā ?	هل يمكن أن أقيس هذا ؟
- Where is the fitting room ?	Ayna Ḥujrat al-qiyās?	أين حجرة القياس ؟
- Is there a mirror ?	Hal tujad mirāyah ?	هل توجد مراية ؟
- Have you a larger size ?	Hal 'indak maqās akbar ?	هل عندك مقاس أكبر ؟

- Do you have the same in black ?	Hal 'indak loon aswad ?	هل عندك لون أسود ؟
- Can you repair this shoes ?	Hal yumkin iŞlāH hāthā al-'Hethā' ?	هل يمكن إصلاح هـــذا الحذاء؟
- I don't understand.	Anā lā afham.	أنا لا أفهم .
- I understand.	Anā afham.	أنا أفهم .
- Can you show me	Mumkin an turiyani?	ممكن أن تريني . . . ؟
- Can you tell me ?	Mumkin taqool li ?	ممكن تقول لي . . . ؟
- Can you help me ?	Mumkin tusā-'idni	ممكن تساعدني ؟
- Can you bring it for me ?	Mumkin tu'Hdhirhā li?	ممكن تحضرها لي ؟
- Please give me.	Min fadhlik a-'aTini	من فضلك أعطني . . .
- I want this.	Urid hāthihi	أريد هذه .
- I don't want this.	Anā lā urid hāthihi	أنا لا أريد هذه .
- Is there another kind ?	Hal yoojad naw'a ākhar	هل يوجد نوع آخر ؟
- I want it cheaper.	Uriduhu rakheiŞ	أريده رخيص .
- I want it smaller.	Uriduhu aŞghar.	أريده أصغر .
- I want it larger.	Uriduhu akbar.	أريده أكبر .

Taxi

- Where can I get a taxi ?	Ayna ajid taxi ?	اين أجد تأكسى ؟
- What is the fare to . . . ?	Kam al-Ujrah ila ?	كم الاجرة الى ...؟
- How far is it to . . ?	Kam al-masāfah ila?	كم المسافة الى ...؟
- Take me to this address.	Khuthni ila hāthā al-'inwān.	خذنى الى هذا العنوان
- Stop here please.	Qif hunā lau sama'Ht	قف هنا لو سمحت
- Could you drive slowly ?	Min fadhlik sooq 'ala mahlak.	من فضلك سوق على مهلك
- Could you help me to carry my bag ?	Hal tusā'idni fi 'Haml 'Haqāi'bi ?	هل تساعدنى فى حمل حقائبى؟
- I want a porter.	Urid shayyāl	أريد شيال..
- Take these bags to.	Khuth hāthihi al-'Haqāi'b ila . . .	خذ هذه الحقائب الى ..
-Take this.	Khuth hāthā.	خذ هذا
- Leave this.	Utruk hāthā.	اترك هذا

66

| - There is one piece missing. | Nāqiṣ qiṬ'ah | . ناقص قطعة |
| - Please I am in a hurry. | Anā must'agil, arjook. | . أنا مستعجل أرجوك |

At the Bank

- Where is the nearest bank ?	Ayna aqrab bank ?	أين أقرب بنك ؟
- . . . currency exchange ?	. . . maktab Şirāfah?	. . .مكتب صرافة ؟
- I want to change some dollars.	Urid taghyeir ba-'adh al-dolarāt.	أريد تغيير بعض الدولارات .
- What is the change rate ?	Mā si-'er al-taʿHweil?	ما سعر التحويل ؟
- Can you cash a personal cheque ?	Hal taŞrif shikāt khāŞah ?	هل تصرف شيكات خاصة؟
- I have a letter of credit.	'Indi khiȚāb dhamān.	عندى خطاب ضمان .
- I am expecting some money.	Anā muntażir floos.	أنا منتظر فلوس .
- Please give me some small change	Min fadhlik a-'aȚini b'adh al-fakkah.	من فضلك أعطنى بعض الفكة
- Give me a large notes.	Min fadhlik a-'aȚini waraqah min fia'h kabirah.	من فضلك أعطنى ورقة من فئة كبيرة .
- Could you please check that again ?	Min fadhlik rāj'e hāthā.	من فضلك راجع هذا .

- I want to credit this to my account.

Urid iydā'a hāthā fi 'Hisābi.

أريد إيداع هذا فى حسابى .

- Where should I sign ?

Ayna Uwaq'i ?

أين أوقع .

* * *

Laundry & Ironing

- Where is the nearest laundry ?	Ayna aqrab maʿHal ghaseil ?	أين أقرب محل غسيل ؟
- I want these clothes ironed	Urid kayy hāthihi al-malābis.	أريد كي هذه الملابس .
- I want cleaning these clothes.	Urid tanżif hāthihi al-malābis.	أريد تنظيف هذه الملابس .
- I want them tomorrow	Uriduhum ghadan.	أريدهم غدا .
- Before Saturday.	Qabla yum al-sabt.	قبل يوم السبت .
- Can you sew on this button ?	Hal yumkinuk an takheiṬ hāthā al-zurār ?	هل يمكنك أن تخيط هذا الزرار ؟
- Can you get this stain out ?	Hal yumkin izālat hāthihi al-buq'ah ?	هل يمكن إزالة هذه البقعة ؟
- Can this be manded ?	Hal yumkin raffat hāthā ?	هل يمكن رفة هذا ؟
- Is my laundry ready ?	Hal ghaseili jāhiz ?	هل غسيلي جاهز ؟
- There is a hole in this shirt.	Yujad khurm fi hāthā al-qamiṢ.	يوجد خرم في هذا القميص.

At the Hotel

- I'd like a single room.	Urid ghurfah lishakhȘ.	أريد غرفة لشخص .
- I'd like a double room.	Urid ghurfah lishakhȘayn.	أريد غرفة لشخصين .
- I'd like a suite.	Urid janāʿH.	أريد جناح .
- I'd like a room with twin beds.	Urid ghurfah bisareirayn.	أريد غرفة بسريرين .
- A room with bath.	. . . ghurfah lahā ʿHammām.	– غرفة لها حمام .
- A room with balcony.	. . . ghurfah lahā balakoonah.	– غرفة لها بلكونة .
- A room facing the sea.	- tuȚil ʿala al-baʿHr.	– تطل على البحر
	- twājih al-baʿHr.	– تواجه البحر
- A room facing the garden.	- tuȚil ʿala al-ʿHadeiqah.	– تطل على الحديقة .
- It must be quiet.	Lā bud an takoon hādi-aʿh.	لا بد أن تكون هادئة .
- Air-conditioned room.	ʿHujrah mukayyafah	حجرة مكيفة .
- A room with TV.	ʿHujrah bi television.	حجرة بتليفزيون .
- A private toilet in	Bihā tawalit khāȘ.	بها تواليت خاص .

71

it.

- A hot and cold water in it.	Bihā mā' sākhin wa bārid.	بها ماء ساخن وبارد .
- What is the price ?	kam al-thaman ?	كم الثمن ؟
Per night ?	Li-laylah ?	لليلة ؟ ..
Per week ?	li-usboo'a?	لأسبوع ؟
- For full board ?	Li- iqāmah kāmilah?	لإقامة كاملة ؟
- Excluding meals.	Bidoon wajabāt	بدون وجبات . ..
Is there any reduction ?	Hal yujad ayy takhfeidh ?	هل يوجد أى تخفيض ؟
- That is too expensive.	Hāthā ghāli jiddan.	هذا غال جدا
- Have you anything cheaper ?	Hal 'indak shaye' arkhaŞ ?	هل عندك شئ أرخص ؟
- For one night only	Lilaylah wāḤidah.	لليلة واحدة .
- At least a week.	Usboo'a 'ala al-aqal.	أسبوع على الأقل .
- Can I see the room?	Mumkin a'ra al-ghurfah	ممكن أرى الغرفة ؟
- I don't like it.	I'nnhā lā tu-'ajibuni.	إنها لا تعجبنى .
- I'd like another room.	Urid Ḥujrah Ukhra.	أريد حجرة أخرى .

- I'll take it.	Sa-ākhuthuhā	. ساخذها
- What is my room number ?	Mā raqam ʹHujrati?	ما رقم حجرتي ؟
- Will you have our bags sent ?	Min fadhlik arsil al-ʹHaqāiʹb	من فضلك أرسل الحقائب .
- Where is the room maid ?	Ayna khādimatu al-ʹHujrah ?	أين خادمة الحجرة ؟
- May I have ash tray please ?	Min fadhlik Ṭaffāyit sagāyer.	من فضلك طفاية سجاير
- Also bath towel.	Wa aydhan fooṬat ʹHammām.	وأيضا فوطة حمام
- Extra pillow	Mikhaddah ziyādah	مخدة زيادة
- Extra blanket	BaṬāniyyah zyādah.	بطانية زيادة
- Writing paper	Waraq kitābah.	ورق للكتابة .
- Where is the bar ?	Ayna al-bār ?	أين البار ؟
- There is no hot water.	Lā yujad māʼ sākhin.	لا يوجد ماء ساخن .
- The lamp is burnt out.	Lambat al-noor maʹHrooqah	لمبة النور محروقة .
- Can you get fixed ?	Hal yumkin islāʹHuhā?	هل يمكن إصلاحها ؟
- Is there any letters for me ?	Hal yujad ayy khitābāt li ?	هل يوجد أى خطابات لى ؟

- Is there is any message for me ?	Hal hunāk ayy rasāi'l li ?	هل هناك أى رسائل لى؟
- May I have my bill?	Mumkin fātoorat 'Hisābi ?	ممكن فاتورة حسابى ؟
- I am leaving tomorrow morning.	Sa-ar'Hal Şabā'H al-ghad.	سأرحل صباح الغد
- I must leave at once.	Lā bud an ar'Hal fawran.	لابد أن أرحل فورا .
- Here is my address.	Hāthā huwa 'inwāny.	هذا هو عنوانى .
Would send some one to bring down **our luggage**	Hal tursil a'Had li inzāl al-'Haqāi'b ?	هل ترسل أحد لإنزال الحقائب ؟
- See you next visit.	Narākum fi zyārah qādimah.	نراكم فى زيارة قادمة .

Eating & Drinking
Out

- Can you recommend me a good resturant?	Min fadhlik inSa'Hni bimaT'am kuwayyis.	من فضلك انصحني مطعم كويس.
- What is the price of the set menu ?	Mā thaman al-wajbah ?	ما ثمن الوجبة ؟
- I'd like an appetizer.	Urid fāti'H shahiyyah	أريد فاتح شهية
- Can you recommend a good meal ?	Mumkin tanSa'Hni bi-a'klah kuwayyisah?	ممكن تنصحني بأكلة كويسة؟
- I'd like some soup.	Urid b'adh al-shurbah.	أريد بعض الشربة.
- What do you command ?	bima ta'mur ?	بم تأمر ؟
- I'd like some fish.	Urid b'adh al-samak.	أريد بعض السمك.
- What kind of sea food do you have ?	Mā anwā-'a al-samak ladayk ?	ما أنواع السمك لديك؟
- What kind of meat do you have ?	Ma anwā-'a al-lu'Hoom ladayk ?	ما أنواع اللحوم لديك ؟

- What vegetable do you have ?	Māthā 'indak min khudhrāwāt ?	ماذا عندك من خضراوات ؟
- I'd like a dessert please.	Urid 'Hulwan min fadhlik.	أزيد حلوا من فضلك .
- Something light.	Shaye' khafeif.	شيئ خفيف .
- Just a small portion.	Miqdār Şagheir.	مقدار صغير .
- What do you have for dessert ?	Ayy anwā-'a al-'Halwa ladaykum	أي أنواع الحلوى لديكم؟
- This is not what I ordered.	Hāthā laysa mā Ţalabtuh.	هذا ليس ما طلبته .
- I cannot eat this.	Lā yumkin an ākul hāthā	لا يمكن أن آكل هذا
- May I change this?	Hal yumkin an Ughayyir hāthā	هل يمكن أن أغير هذا ؟
- It is over done.	Innahu sayyi' jiddan.	إنه سيئ جدا
- Too tough.	Nāshif jiddan	ناشف جدا
- Too sweet.	Misakkar jiddan	مسكر جدا
- Salty.	Māli'H	مالح
- Bitter.	Mur	مر

- It's not fresh.	Laysa Ṭāzah	ليس طازة
- Would you ask the headwaiter to come over ?	UṬlub min al-mitr al-Ḥudhoor min fadhlik	اطلب من المتر الحضور من فضلك .
- I'd like some mineral water.	Urid miyāh ma-'adaniyyah	أريد مياه معدنية .
- I'd like juice.	Urid 'aṢir	أريد عصيرا .
I'd like cheese sandwich.	Urid sandwich jibn	أريد ساندويتش جبن .
- Have you cold drink?	Mumkin Ḥāgah Ṣāq'ah ?	ممكن حاجة صاقعة ؟

Post Office, Telegram & Telephone

- Where is the nearest post office ?	Ayna aqrab maktab. bareid ?	أين أقرب مكتب بريد ؟
- ... telegram office?	... maktab telleghrāf ?	. . . مكتب تلغراف ؟
- What time does it open ?	Mata yuftaH́ ?	متى يفتح ؟
- What window do I go to for stamps ?	Ayna shibbāk al-Ṭwāb'e ?	أين شباك الطوابع ؟
- I want some stamps please.	Urid b'adh al-Ṭwāb'e min fadhlik.	أريد بعض الطوابع من فضلك ؟
- What is the postage for a letter to England ?	Bikam al-khiṬāb lingiltrā ?	بكم الخطاب لإنجلترا ؟
- What a postage for post card to USA ?	mā thaman irsāl kārt bustāl li-amrikā?	ما ثمن إرسال كارت بوستال لأمريكا ؟

78

English	Transliteration	العربية
- Do you send parcels ?	Hal tursil Ṭurood?	هل ترسل طرود ؟
- Where I cash money address ?	Ayna a-'amal 'Hiwālah bareidiyyah?	أين أعمل حوالة بريدية؟
- I want to send this parcel.	Urid irsāl hāthā al-Ṭard.	أريد إرسال هذا الطرد
- Where is the mail box ?	Ayna Ṣandooq al-khiṬābāt ?	أين صندوق الخطابات ؟
- I want to send this letter.	Urid an ursil hāthā al-khiṬāb.	أريد أن أرسل هذا الخطاب.
- By air mail.	- bilbareid al-jawwi.	– بالبريد الجوى .
- By express.	-bilbareid al-mist'ajil	– بالبريد المستعجل .
- By registered mail.	- bilbareid al-musajjal.	– بالبريد المسجل .
- Is there any mail for me ?	Hal tujad khiṬābāt li?	هل توجد خطابات لى ؟
- Here is my passport.	Hāthā bāsburi.	هذا باسبورى .
- I want to send a telegram.	Urid irsāl tellighrāf.	أريد إرسال تلغراف .
- May I have a form?	Mumkin tu-'uṬeini istimārah ?	ممكن تعطينى استمارة ؟

- You gave me a wrong number.	A-'aTaytani nimrah ghalaT.	أعطيتني نمرة غلط .
- How long will a cable to England take ?	Kam yastaghriq al-tellighrāf ila ingiltirah ?	كم يستغرق التلغراف الى إنجلترا ؟
- I'd like to reverse the charge.	Urid an yadfa-'a al-mustalim thaman al-tellighrāf.	أريد أن يدفع المستلم ثمن التلغراف .
- May I use the phone ?	Mumkin astakhdim al-telifoon ?	ممكن أستخدم التليفون ؟
- Do you have a telephone directory?	Hal ladayk daleil telifoon ?	هل لديك دليل تليفون ؟
I want Luxor.	Urid al-UqSur.	أريد الأقصر .
- Can I dial direct.	Hal yujad khaT mubāshir ?	هل يوجد خط مباشر ؟
- I want to place a personal call.	Urid mukālamah shakhSiyyah.	أريد. مكالمة شخصية .
- Will tell me the cost of the call ?	Mā qeimat al-mukālamah ?	ما قيمة المكالمة ؟
- I want to speak to .	Urid an ata'Haddath ila. . .	أريد أن أتحدث الى .
- Would you put me through to ?	• Min fadhlik a-'aTinei	• من فضلك أعطني
—Try again ?	• 'Hāwil marrah ukhra.	• حاول مرة أخرى

- Operator, we were cut off.	Laqad inqaṬʻat al-mukālamah.	لقد انفطعت المكالمة .
- Would you tell her I called ?	Min fadhlik qul lahā anny ittaṢalt.	من فضلك قل لها أني اتصلت .
- Would you ask him to call me ?	Min fadhlik uṬlub minhu an yattaṢil bi	من فضلك اطلب منه أن يتصل بى .
- Would you please take a message ?	Min fadhlik khuth hāthihi al-rislāh.	من فضلك خذ هذه الرسالة .
- I want to pay for the call.	Urid an adfa-ʻa thaman al-mukālamah.	أريد أن أدفع ثمن المكالمة .
- Is the line engaged?	Hal al-khaṬ mashghool ?	هل الخط مشغول ؟

* * *

81

Travelling

- Is there a flight to Luxor ?	Hal tujad ri'Hlah ila al-UkŞur ?	هل توجد رحلة الى الأقصر؟
- When is the next plane to Cairo ?	Mā maw'id al-Ţāi'rah al-qādimah ila al-qāhirah ?	ما موعد الطائرة القادمة الى القاهرة ؟
- Can I make a connection to Alexandria ?	Hal astaŢi'-e an a-'amal imtidād ila al-iskandariyyah ?	هل أستطيع أن أعمل امتداد الى الإسكندرية ؟
- I'd like a ticket to Aswan.	Urid tathkarah ila Aswān.	أريد تذكرة الى أسوان .
- What time does the plane take off ?	Mata taqoom al-Ţāi'rah ?	متى تقوم الطائرة ؟
- What time do I have to check in ?	Mata yajib an atwājad bilmaŢār ?	متى يجب أن أتواجد بالمطار؟
- What is the flight number ?	Mā raqam al-ri'Hlah?	ما رقم الرحلة ؟
- What time do we arrive ?	Mata NaŞil ?	متى نصل ؟

English	Transliteration	العربية
- What bus do I take to Fayyum ?	Ayy Utoobeis arkab ila al-fayyum ?	أى أتوبيس أركب الى الفيوم ؟
- Where is the bus station ?	Ayna mawqif al-Utoobeis ?	أين موقف الأتوبيس ؟
Where is the bus stop ?	Ayna maʿHatat al-Utoobeis ?	أين محطة الأتوبيس ؟
- When is the next bus to Tahrir square?	Mata yaqoom al-utoobeis al-tāli ila Maydān al-TaʿHreir?	متى يقوم الأتوبيس التالى الى ميدان التحرير ؟
- How long does the journey take ?	Mā muddat al-riʿHlah ?	ما مدة الرحلة ؟
- Where is the information office ?	Ayna maktab al-isti-ʿelāmāt ?	أين مكتب الاستعلامات؟
- Where can I buy a ticket ?	Min ayna ashtari tathkarah ?	من أين أشترى تذكرة ؟
- I want a ticket to Sinai ?	Urid tathkarah ila sināʿ .	أريد تذكرة الى سيناء
- How much is the fare to . . . ?	Kam al-ujrah ila . .?	كم الأجرة الى . . . ؟
- One way or round trip ?	Thihāb am thihāb wa iyāb ?	ذهاب أم ذهاب وإياب؟
- Is this seat taken ?	Hal hāthā al-kursi maʿHjooz	هل هذا الكرسى محجوز ؟

English	Transliteration	العربية
- When we get to the Pyramid ?	Mata naŞil ila al-ahrām ?	متى نصل الى الأهرام ؟
- What station is this?	Mā hāthihi al-maʿHaṬah ?	ما هذه المحطة ؟
- Will you tell me when to get off ?	Qul li mata anzil min fadhlik	قل لى متى أنزل من فضلك.
- I want to get off at opera.	Urid al-nuzool fi al-ubrah .	أريد النزول فى الأوبرا .
- Please let me off at the next stop.	Min fadhlik anzil fi al-maʿHaṬah al-tāliyah .	من فضلك أنزل فى المحطة التالية .
- May I have my luggage please ?	Urid shanṬati min fadhlik.	أريد شنطتى من فضلك .
- Where is the railway station ?	Ayna maʿHaṬat al-sikkah al-Ḥadeid ?	أين محطة السكة الحديد ؟
- Take me there.	Khuthni ila hunāk.	خذنى الى هناك .
- Is the train late ?	Hal al-qiṬār mutaʿkhir ?	هل القطار متأخر ؟
- Is there a sleeping car on the train ?	Hal tujad ʾarabat noom fi al-qiṬār ?	هل توجد عربة نوم فى القطار ؟
- . . . dining car ?	. . . ʾarbat Ṭa-ʾām?	. . . عربة طعام ؟

84

- What platform does the train leave from ?	Min ayy raŞeif yaqoom al-qiŢār ?	من أى رصيف يقوم القطار؟
- First or second class do you want ?	Darjah u'-ola am thāniyah tureid ?	درجة أولى أم ثانية تريد ؟
–Where is the ticket office ?	Ayna maktab al-tathākir ?	أين مكتب التذاكر ؟
- This the ticket office.	Hāthā shubbāk al-tathākir.	هذا شباك التذاكر .
- This is a waiting hall.	Hāthihi Şālat intiżār.	هذه صالة انتظار .
- Where is the next steamer sailing to ?	ila ayna sa-tub'Hir al-bākhirah al-tāliyah?	إلى أين ستبحر الباخرة التالية ؟
- Where is the tourist office ?	Ayna maktab al-siyā'Hah ?	أين مكتب السياحة ؟
- What are the main points of interest ?	Mā hiya aham al-m'ālim al-siyā'Hiyyah ?	ما هى أهم المعالم السياحية ؟
- Where does the bus start from ?	Min ayna yaqoom al-utoobeis ?	من أين يقوم الأتوبيس ؟
- Will it pick us up at the hotel ?	Hal sa-ya'khuthunā min al-funduq ?	هل سيأخذنا من الفندق؟
- How much does the tour cost ?	Kam tukalleif al-ri'Hlah ?	كم تكلف الرحلة ؟

-I'd like to rent a car.	Ureid ta'jeir sayyārah.	أريد تأجير سيارة .
- Is the museum opening today ?	Hal al-matʿHaf maftooʿH al-yum ?	هل المتحف مفتوح اليوم؟
- When does it close	Mata yughlaq ?	متى يغلق ؟
- How much is the admission charge ?	Bikam al-dukhool ?	بكم الدخول ؟
- Have you a catalogue ?	Hal 'indak kataloog?	هل عندك كتالوج ؟
- Have you post cards ?	Hal 'indak kroot ?	هل عندك كروت ؟
- Can I take a picture ?	Mumkin ākhuth Şoorah ?	ممكن آخذ صورة ؟
- What is that building ?	Mā hāthā al-mabna?	ما هذا المبنى ؟
- Where is the house where Nassir lived ?	Ayna al-manzil allathi 'āsh fihi 'abd el-NāŞir ?	أين المنزل الذى عاش فيه عبد الناصر ؟
- Is there any reduction ?	Hal yujad ayy takhfeidh?	هل يوجد أى تخفيض ؟

Cars & Roads

- Where is the next gas station ?	Ayna aqrab ma'Ha Tat banzein ?	أين أقرب محطة بنزين ؟
- I want 5 litters of petrol please.	Ureid khamsat litrāt min fadhlik.	أريد خمسة لترات بنزين من فضلك .
- Give me one litter of oil.	A-'aTini litr zeit.	أعطني لتر زيت .
- Can you mend this puncture ?	Min fadhlik aSli'H hāthihi al-'ajalah.	من فضلك أصلح هذه العجلة .
- Check the brake fluid,	Ikshif 'ala al-farāmil.	اكشف على زيت الفرامل .
- Please check the oil and water.	Min fadhlik ikshif 'ala al-zeit wa al-mayyah.	من فضلك اكشف على الزيت والميه .
- Would you change this tire please ?	Mumkin taghayyeir hāthihi al-'ajalah min fadhlik ?	ممكن تغيير هذه العجلة من فضلك ؟
- Will you clean the wind screen ?	Mumkin tunażif al-zujaj al-amāmi	ممكن تنظف الزجاج الأمامى؟
- Have you a road map ?	'Indak khareiTat Turuq?	عندك خريطة طرق ؟
- Can you tell me	Mumkin taqool li	ممكن تقول لى الطريق الى ؟

87

the way to ,,, ?	al-Ṭareiq ila . . .?	الى أين يؤدى هذا الطريق ؟
- Where does this road lead to ?	Ila ayna yuaʿddei hāthā al-Ṭareiq ?	
- How far is it to Cairo ?	Kam al-masāfah ila al-qāhirah ?	كم المسافة الى القاهرة ؟
- Go straight ahead.	Sir 'ala Ṭool .	سر على طول .
- This is my driving license.	Hāthihi rukhṢat al-qiyādah.	هذه رخصة القيادة .
- May I park here ?	Mumkin arkin hunā?	ممكن أركن هنا ؟
- What is the charge for parking here ?	Kam ujrat al-garāj hunā ?	كم أجرة الجراج هنا ؟
- The road is narrow .	Al-Ṭareiq dhayyiq.	الطريق ضيق .
- No parking.	Mamnoo-'a al-intiżar.	ممنوع الانتظار .
- No entry.	Mamnoo-'a al-dukhool.	ممنوع الدخول ..
- Dangerous bend.	Mun'Hana khaṬeir.	منحنى خطير .
- Keep right.	Ilzam al-yamein.	الزم اليمين .
- Level crossing.	Mazlaqān	مزلقان
- Where is the nearest garage ?	Ayna aqrab garāj ?	أين أقرب جراج
- My car has broken down.	Sayyrāratei t'aṬalat.	سيارتى تعطلت .
- Can you send a	Hal tursil li	هل ترسل لى ميكانيكى ؟

88

mechanic ?	mikāneikei?	
- I don't know what is wrong with it.	Anā lā a-'arif mā bihā.	٠أنا لا أعرف ما بها .
- The car does not start.	Al-syyārah lā tadoor.	السيارة لا تدور .
- The car does not pull.	Al-sayyārah lā tas'Hab.	السيارة لا تسحب .
- The car making a funny noise ?	Al- sayyārah bihā Şawt ghareib.	السيارة بها صوت غريب .
- It is locked and the key inside.	Al-sayyārah maqfoolah wa al-miftā'H bidākhilihā.	السيارة مقفولة والمفتاح بداخلها .
- The radiator is leaking.	Al-radyāteir yakhur.	الرادياتير يخر .
- The clutch disengages too quickly .	Al-dibriyāj yaflit bisur'ah.	الدبرياج يفلت بسرعة
- The steering wheel is vibrating.	'Ajalat al-qiyādah tahtaz.	عجلة القيادة تهتز
- Can I leave my car here ?	Hal astaŢi-'e an atruk sayyārati hunā ?	هل أستطيع أن أترك سيارتى هنا ؟
- Is everything fixed?	Hal tam işlā'H kul shaye'	هل تم إصلاح كل شئ ؟

89

Chapter Four

Verbs

- The verb differs (in writing and pronunciation) according to the pronoun used.
- Read the following forms of the verb to know the difference.

Went out	Kharaja	خرج
Ali went out	'Ali Kharaja	علي خرج
Muna went out	Muna Kharajat	مني خرجت
Ali and Ahmed went out	'Ali wa A'Hmad Kharajā.	علي وأحمد خرجا
Muna and Huda went out.	Muna wa Huda kharajatā	مني وَهدى خرجتا
Pupils went out	Al-talāmeith kharajoo	التلاميذ خرجوا
The girls went out	Al-banāt kharajna	البنات خرجن

In Arabic the verb is classified into three tenses :

Past tense	Mādhi	ماضي
Present tense	Mudhār'a	مضارع
Command	Amr	أمر

93

- Study the following examples to know the verb in present tense (mudhār'a مضارع)

Go out	Yakhruju	يخرج
Ali goes out	'Ali yakhruju	علی يخرج
Muna goes out	Muna takhruju	منى تخرج
Ali and Ahmed go out	'Ali wa A'Hmad yakhrujān	علی و أحمد يخرجان
Muna and Huda go out	Muna wa Huda takhrujān	منى و هدى تخرجان
Pupils go out	Al-Talāmeith yakhrujoon	التلاميذ يخرجون
The **girls** go out	Al-Banāt yakhrujna	البنات يخرجن

- Study the following examples to know the command verb (Amr أمر)

Go out Ali	Ukhruj yā 'Ali	اخرج يا علی
Go out Muna	Ukhruji yā Muna	اخرجی يا منى
Go out Ali and Ahmed	'Ali wa A'Hmad Ukhrujā	علی و أحمد اخرجا

94

| Pupils, go out | Yā talāmeith ukhrujoo | يا تلاميذ اخرجوا |
| Girls, go out | Yā banāt ukhrujna | يا بنات اخرجن |

* * *

More examples :

Past Tense	Al-Māḍhi	الماضي
Hamid went to school.	'Hāmid thahaba ila al-madrasah	حامد ذهب الى المدرسة
Samir understood the lesson.	Sameir fahima al-dars.	سمير فهم الدرس
The child drank the milk.	Al-Ṭifl shariba al-laban.	الطفل شرب اللبن
The teacher explained the lesson.	Al-mudarris sharaʻHa al-dars.	المدرس شرح الدرس
My father wrote a letter to my brother	Wālidi kataba khiṬāban ila akhi.	والدى كتب خطابا الى أخى

Notice

The verbs فهم (fahima), شرب (shariba), شرح (sharaʻHa), كتب (kataba), must have "fat-Hah" ( ) over the last letter.

* * *

95

Present Tense	Al-Mudhāhr'a	المضارع
Hamid goes to school.	'Hāmid yath–habu ila al-madrasah	حامد يذهب الى المدرسة
Samir understands the lesson.	Samir yafhamu al-dars.	سمير يفهم الدرس .
The child drinks the milk	Al-Ţifl yashrabu al-laban.	الطفل يَشرب اللبن
The teacher explains the lesson.	Al-mudarris yashra'Hu al-dars.	المدرس يشرح الدرس
My father writes a letter to my brother.	Wālidi yaktubu khiŢāban ila akhi.	أبى يكتب خطابا الى أخى .

Notice

The verbs يذهب (yath–habu), يفهم (yafhamu), and يشرب (yashrabu) must have a dhammah ( ) over the last letter.

* * *

96

The Command Sentence	Jumlat al-Amr	جملة الأمر
Hamid, go to school.	ʹHāmid, Ith-hab ila al-madrasah.	حامد ، اذهب الى المدرسة
Samir, study the lesson	Sameir, istathkir al-dars	سمير استذكر الدرس .
Kamil, go to the field.	Kāmil, ith-hab ila al-ʹHaql,	كامل ، اذهب الى الحقل
Samah, clean the office.	Naẓẓifi al-maktab yā SamāʹH.	نظفى المكتب يا سماح .

Notice

The verbs اذهب (iżhab), and استذكر (istażkir) must have

sukoun ( ) over the last letter.

* * *

There are some important verbs in different tenses :

To go out	يخرج' Yakhruju	خرج Kharaja	أخرج Ukhruj
To enter	يدخل' Yadkhulu	دخل Dakhala	أدخل Udkhul

To sit down	يجلس' Yajlisu	جلس Jalasa	اجلس Ijlis
To stand up	يقف' Yaqifu	وقف Waqafa	قف Qif
To play	يلعب' Yal'abu	لعب La-'iba	العب Il'ab
To study	يستذكر' Yastathkiru	استذكر Istathkara	استذكر Istathkir
To sleep	ينام' Yanāmu	نام Nāma	نم Näm
To wake up	يستيقظ' Yastayqiżu	استيقظ Istayqaża	استيقظ Istayqiż
To run	يجرى Yajri	جرى Jara	اجر Ijre
To eat	يأكل' Ya'kulu	أكل a'kala	كل Kul
To drink	يشرب' Yashrabu	شرب Shariba	اشرب Ishrab
To read	يقرأ Yaqra-u'	قرأ Qara'	اقرأ Iqra'

98

To write	يكتب	كتب	اكتب
	Yaktubu	Kataba	Uktub
To speak	يتكلم	تكلم	تكلم
	Yatakallamu	Takallama	Takallam
To work	يعمل	عمل	اعمل
	Y'amalu	'Amala	I-'emal
To cook	يطبخ	طبخ	اطبخ
	YaṬbukhu	Ṭabakha	UṬbukh
To wash	يغسل	غسل	اغسل
	Yaghsilu	Ghasala	Ighsil
To arrange	يرتب	رتب	رتب
	Yurattibu	Rattaba	Rattib
To open	يفتح	فتح	افتح
	Yafta′Hu	Fata′Ha	Ifta′H
To close	يغلق	أغلق	اغلق
	Yughliqu	Aghlaqa	Aghliq
To drive	يسوق	ساق	سق
	Yasooqu	Sāqa	Suq
To clean	ينظف	نظف	نظف
	Yunaẓẓifu	Naẓẓafa	Naẓẓif

To remember	يتذكر	تذكر	تذكر
	Yatathakkaru	Tathakkara	Tathakkar
To forget	ينسى	نسى	انس
	Yansa	Nasiya	Insä
To try	يحاول	حاول	حاول
	Yu'Hāwilu	'Hāwala	'Hāwil
To leave	يغادر	غادر	غادر
	Yughādiru	Ghādara	Ghādir
To return	يعود	عاد	عد
	Ya-'ūdu	'Ādä	'Ud
To die	يـموت	مات	مت
	Yamootu	Mata	Mut
To live	يعيش	عاش	عش
	Ya-'eishu	'Aāsha	'Ish
To kill	يقتل	قتل	إقتل
	Yaqtulu	Qatala	Uqtul

To know	يعرف' Y'arifu	عرف 'Aarafa	اعرف I-'eraf
To look	ينظر' Yanżuru	نظر Nażara	انظر Unżur
To walk	يمشى Yamshi	مشى Masha	امش Imshe
To tell	يخبر' Yukhbiru	أخبر Akhbara	اخبر Akhbir
To wait	ينتظر' Yantażeru	انتظر Intażara	انتظر Intażir
To build	يبنى Yabni	بنى Bana	ابن Ibne
To prepare	يجهز' Yujahhizu	جهز Jahhaza	جهز Jahhiz
To think	يفكر' Yufakkiru	فكر Fakkara	فكر Fakkir
To buy	يشترى Yashtari	اشترى Ishtara	اشتر Ishtare

To sell	يبيع yabi'e	باع Bā-'a	بع Bi-'e
To change	يغير Yughayyir	غير Ghayyara	غير Ghayyir
To travel	يسافر Yusāfiru	سافر Sāfara	سافر Sāfir
To receive	يستقبل Yastaqbilu	استقبل Istaqbala	استقبل Istaqbil
To meet	يقابل Yuqābilu	قابل Qābala	قابل Qābil
To serve	يخدم Yakhdumu	خدم Khadama	اخدم Ikhdim
To help	يساعد Yusā-'idu	ساعد Sā-'ada	ساعد Sā-'id
To succeed	ينجح Yanja'Hu	نجح Naja'Ha	انجح Inja'H
To fail	يرسب Yarsubu	رسب Rasaba	ارسب Ursub
To sing	يغني Yughanni	غنى Ghanna	غن Ghanne

102

To dance	يرقص' Yarquşu	رقص RaqaŞa	ارقص UrquŞ
To explain	يشرح' Yashra'Hu	شرح Shara'Ha	اشرح Ishra'H
To understand	يفهم' Yafhamu	فهم Fahima	افهم Ifham
To take	يأخذ' Ya'khuthu	أخذ Akhatha	خذ Khuth
To give	يعطى Y'uŢi	أعطى A-'aŢa	أعط A-'aŢi
To dream	يحلم' Ya'Hlumu	حلم 'Halama	احلم Ihlam
To watch	يراقب' Yurāqibu	راقب Rāqaba	راقب Rāqib
To rest	يستريح Yastarei'Hu	استراح Istrā'Ha	استرح Istari'H
To laugh	يضحك Yadh-'Haku	ضحك Dha'Hika	اضحك Idh-'Hak
To win	يكسب Yaksabu	كسب Kasiba	اكسب Iksab

To lose	يَخسَر Yakhsaru	خسِر Khasira	إخسَر Ikhsar
To repair	يصلح YuṢliʼHu	أصلح AṢlaʼHa	اصلح AṢliʼH
To agree	يوافق Yuwāfiqu	وافق Wāfaqa	وافق Wāfiq
To refuse	يرفضْ Yarfudhu	رفض Rafadha	ارفض Urfudh
To visit	يزورْ Yazooru	زار Zāra	زُرْ Zur

- In the Past Tense الفعل الماضى we put "fat-hah" (´) over the last letter. For example the verbs خرَجَ and ذاكـرَ gramatically we say Kharaja and Thākara, but in colloquial language we say ذاكـر (Thākar) and خرج (Kharaj)

- In the Present Tense الفعل المضارع we put Dammah (´) over the last letter. Grammatically we say يذاكرْ (Yuthākiru) and يَخرُج (Yakhruju). In this case the last letter must not be Yā' (ي) or Alif (ا)

- There are some letters (not necessary to know them now) if they come before the Present Tense الفعل المضارع al-dhammah (ُ) is to be changed into fat-hah ( ).

- Also there are some letters which change it into sukoon (ْ).

- Al-sukoon (ْ) must be over the last letter in case of the Commnd Verb فعل الأمـــر, or when some certain letters come before the Present Tense. But in both cases if the last letter is wāw (و) , Yā' (ي) or Alif (ا) you should omit these letters and not put sukoon (ْ) over them. For example the Command Verbs from the ensuing verbs is formed as follows :

Ijre	أجر	يجرى
Imshe	امش	يمشى
Ibne	ابن	يبنى

105

Ishtare	اشتر	يشترى	
Ghanne	غن	يغنى	
A-'a Ṭe	أعط	يعطى	

* * *

Don't run	Lā Tajre	لا تجر
He doesn't build	Lam yabne	لم يبن
He doesn't come nearer	Lam Yadnu	لم يدن

Chapter Five

Pronouns

- Pronouns are classified into Subject Pronouns ضمائر الفاعل
  (Dhamā'-ir al-Fā-'il), Object Pronouns ضمائر المفعـــول
  (Dhamā'-ir al-Maf'ūl), and Possessive Pronouns ضمائر
  الملكية (Dhamā'-ir al-Milkiyyah).
- Each of these three types are subdivided into :
A) First Person Pronouns ضمـائر المتكلــم (Dhamā'-ir al-
   Mutakallim) ,
B) Second Person Pronouns ضمائر المخـــاطب (Dhamāi'-r al-
   Mukhāṭab),
C) and Third Person Pronouns ضمائر الغائب (Dhamāi'r al-
   Ghāi'b) .

- Regarding gender, pronouns are divided into male and
  female

  *   *   *

ضمائر الفاعل

(Dhamāi'-r al-Fā'-il)

Subject Pronouns

● ضمائر الفاعل المتكلم

● **Subject First Person Pronouns**

١. ضمير الفاعل المتكلم المفرد

(مذكر أو مؤنث)

Subject First Person Singular Pronoun

I	Anā	<div dir="rtl">أَـــا</div>

Ex. I met Ali	Anā qābaltu 'Ali	<div dir="rtl">قابلت على</div>

٢. ضمير الفاعل المتكلم الجمع

(مذكر أو مؤنث)

Subject First Person Plural Pronoun

We	NaʼHnu	<div dir="rtl">نحن</div>

110

Ex. We met Ali	Na'Hnu qābalnā 'Ali	نحن قابلنا على

- Subject Second Person Pronouns

ضمائر الفاعل المخاطب

Second Person Male Singular Pronoun

١ . ضمير الفاعل المخاطب المذكر

المفرد

| You | Anta | أنت |

| You shall leave | Anta satar'Hal | أنت سترحل |

Second Person Female Pronoun

٢ . ضمير الفاعل المخاطب المؤنث

المفرد

| You | Anti | أنت |

| You shall leave | Anti sa'ar'Halein | أنت سترحلين |

111

<u>Second Person Male/Female</u>
(two person) Pronoun

٣ . ضمير المخاطب المثنى (المذكر

والمؤنث)

You   Antumā   أنتما

| You have succeeded | Antuma naja'Htumā | أنتما نجحتما |

<u>Second Person Male Plural</u>
Pronoun

٤ . ضمير المخاطب الجمع المذكر

You   Antum   أنتم

| You shall leave | Antum sa-tar'Haloon | أنتم سترحلون |

<u>Second Person Female</u>
Plural Pronoun

٥ . ضمير المخاطب الجمع المؤنث

You   Antunna   أنتن

112

You shall leave	Antunna sa-tar'Halna	أنتن سترحلن

* * *

Subject Third Person Pronouns

● ضمائر الفاعل الغائب

Third Person Male Singular Pronoun

١ . ضمير الفاعل الغائب المذكر المفرد

He   Huwa   هو

He has understood the lesson	Huwa fahima al-dars	هو فهم الدرس

Third Person Female Singular Pronoun

٢ . ضمير الفاعل الغائب المؤنث المفرد

She   Hiya   هى

She has understood the lesson	Hiya fahimat al-dars	هى فهمت الدرس

Third Person Male/Female (two persons) Pronoun

٣ . ضمير الفاعل الغائب المثنى المذكر

أو المؤنث

They	Humā		هما
They killed him	Humā qatalāh (for male) Huma qatalatāh (for female)	(for male) (for female)	هما قتلاه هما قتلتاه

Third Person Male Plural Pronoun

٤ . ضمير الفاعل الغائب الجمع المذكر

They	Hum		هم
They visited him	Hum zārooh		هم زاروه

Third Person Female Plural Pronoun

٥ . ضمير الفاعل الغائب الجمع المؤنث

They	Hunna		هن
They visited him	Hunna zurnahu		هن زرنه

ضمائر المفعول

Dhamā'-ir Al- Maf'ūl
Object Pronouns

- Object pronouns may be the object of a verb or a preposition.
- These prounouns are also different according to number and gender. For explanation, study the verb قابل (qābala) which means "met" with the various object pronouns.

Ali met me	'Ali qābalani	علی قابلنـــــی
Ali met us	'Ali qābalanā	علی قابلـنـــا
Ali met you	'Ali qābalaka	علی قابلـك
Ali met you (female)	'Ali qābalaki	علی قابلـك
Ali met you (two person male/female)	'Ali qābalakumā	علی قابلـكــما
Ali met you (male/plural)	'Ali qābalakum	علی قابلـكــم
Ali met you (female/plural)	'Ali qābalakunna	علی قابلـكن
Ali met him	'Ali qābalahu	علی قابلــه

Ali met her	'Ali qābalahā	على قابلـــها
Ali met them (male/female two persons)	'Ali qābalahumā	على قابلـــهما
Ali met them (male/plural)	'Ali qābalahum	على قابلـــهم
Ali met them (female/plural	'Ali qābalahunna	على قابلـــهن

* * *

ضمائر الملكية

Dhamā'-ir Al-Milkiyyah
Possessive Pronouns

These prounouns are also different according to number and gender. For explanation, study the word كتاب (kit**ā**b) which means "book" with various possessives.

My book (m/f)	Kit**ā**b**ei**	كتابـــــى
Our book (m/f)	Kit**ā**bun**ā**	كتابـــنا
Your book (m/s)	Kit**ā**bu**k**a	كتابـك
Your book (f/s)	Kit**ā**bu**k**i	كتابـك ;
Your book (m/f two person)	Kit**ā**bu**kumā**	كتابـكما
Your book (m/p)	Kit**ā**bu**kum**	كتابـكم
Your book (f/p)	Kit**ā**bu**kunna**	كتابـكن
His book	Kit**ā**bu**hu**	كتابـــه
Her book	Kit**ā**bu**hā**	كتابها
Their book (m/f two persons)	Kit**ā**bu**humā**	كتابـــهما

117

| Their book (m/p) | **Kitābuhum** | كتابــهم |
| Their book (f/p) | **Kitābuhunna** | كتابــهن |

Chapter Six

Interrogative Words

Why ?	Limāthā ? (Lih ?)	لماذا ؟ (ليه ؟)
Ex. Why do you go to school ?	Limāthā tāth-habu ila al-madrasah ?	لماذا تذهب الى المدرسة ؟

What ?	Māthā ? Ma? (Iyh ?)	ماذا ؟ ما ؟ (إيه ؟)
Ex. - What are you writing	Māthā taktubu ?	ماذا تكتب ؟
- What is your name ?	- Mā Ismuk ? - Ismak iyh ?	– ما اسمك ؟ – (اسمك إيه ؟)
- What is the matter ?	- Māthā Ḥadath ? - Iyh illi ḤaṢal ?	ماذا حدث ؟ (إيه اللى حصل ؟)

Where ?	Ayna ? (Fein ?)	أين ؟ (فين ؟)
Ex. Where have you been ?	- Ayna Kunt ? - Kunt (fein)	– أين كنت ؟ (– كنت فين ؟)

When ?	Mata ? (Imta ?)	متى ؟ (إمته ؟)
Ex. When will you travel ?	- Mata satusāfir ? - (Imata ´Hatsāfir ?)	– متى ستسافر ؟ (– إمته حتسافر ؟)

Which ?	Ayy ?	أى ؟
Ex. Which book do you want	Ayy kitāb turid ?	أى كتاب تريد ؟

Whose ?	Liman ?	لمن ؟
Ex. Whose car is this ?	Liman hāthihi al-sayyārah ?	لمن هذه السيارة ؟

122

How ?	Kayfa ? (Izzāy ?)	كيف ؟ (إزاي ؟)
Ex. How do you go to the airport ?	- Kayfa tath-hab ila al-maȚār ? - Izzāy troo'Hal-maȚār?	– كيف تذهب الى المطار ؟ – (إزاى تروح المطار ؟)
From where ?	Min Ayna (Minein)	من أين ؟ (منين ؟)
Ex. Where did you bring the book from ?	- Min ayna a'Hdhart al-kitāb? - Minein gibt al-kitab	– من أين أحضرت الكتاب؟ – (منين جبت الكتاب ؟)
From what ?	Mimmā ?	مما ؟
Ex. From what does water consist ?	- Mimmā yatakawwan al-mā'	– مم يتكون الماء ؟
Who ?	Män ? (Mein)	مَنْ ؟ (مين ؟)
Ex. Who built the	- Män bana al-	

pyramids ?	ahrām ? - (Mein illi bana al-ahrām ?)	؟ من بنى الأهرام – (؟ مين اللى بنى الأهرام) –
How many ? How much ? How old ? How long ? How far? etc.	Kam ?	؟ كم
Ex. - How many books have you bought	- Kam Kitaban Ishtarayt ?	؟ كم كتابا اشتريت –
- How old are you?	- Kam 'Umruk ?	؟ كم عمرك –
- How long did you stay in Cairo ?	- Kam makathta fi al-Qāhirah ?	؟ كم مكثت فى القاهرة –
- How far it is beween Cairo and Fayyoom?	- Kam al-masāfah bayna al-Qāhirah wa al-Fayyoom ?	كم المسافة بين القاهرة – ؟ والفيوم
- How high is the Pyramid ?	- Kam irtifā'a al-haram ?	؟ كم ارتفاع الهرم –

Chapter Seven

Time, Numbers,

Time

الزمـــــن
Al-Zamän

● **Seasons of the Year.**	FuŞool al-Sanah.	فصول السنة
Spring	Al-rabei:a	ربيع
Summer	Al-Şayf	الصيف
Autumn	Al-khareif	الخريف
Winter	Al-shitā'	الشتاء
● **Months of the Year**	Shuhoor al-Sanah	شهور السنة
January	Yanāyir	يناير
February	Fibrāyir	فبراير
March	Māris	مارس
April	Abreil	ابريل

May	Māyoo	مايو
June	Yunyah	يونيه
July	Yulyah	يوليه
August	AghusṬus	أغسطس
September	Sibtamber	سبتمبر
October	Uktoober	أكتوبر
November	Noofamber	نوفمبر
December	Deisamber	ديسمبر

● Days of the week.	Ayyām al-Usboo-'a	أيام الأسبوع
Saturday	Al-Sabt	السبت
Sunday	Al-A'Had	الأحد
Monday	Al-Ithnein	الإثنين
Tuesday	Al-Thulāthā'	الثلاثاء
Wednesday	Al-Arba-'ā'	الأربعاء
Thursday	Al-Khameis	الخميس
Friday	Al-Jum'ah	الجمعة

الساعة Hour

An hour	Sā- ʼah	ساعة
A minute	Daqeiqah	دقيقة
A second	Thānyah	ثانية

* * *

Numbers الأعــــداد

0	Şifr	.	صفر
1	Wā'Hid	١	واحد
2	Ithnān	٢	اثنان
3	Thalāthah	٣	ثلاثة
4	Arba-'ah	٤	أربعة
5	Khamsah	٥	خمسة
6	Sittah	٦	ستة
7	Sab'ah	٧	سبعة
8	Thamāniyah	٨	ثمانية
9	Tis'ah	٩	تسعة
10	'Ashrah	١٠	عشرة
11	- IHda 'ashar - (Hidāshar)	١١	– أحد عشر – (حداشر)
12	-Ithna 'ashar - (Itnāshar)	١٢	– اثنا عشر – (اتناشر)

130

13	- Thalāthat 'ashar	١٣	– ثلاثة عشر
	- (Talattāshar)		– (تلتاشر)
14	- Arb'at 'ashar	١٤	– أربعة عشر
	- (Arb'atāshar)		– (أربعتاشر)
15	- Khamsat 'ashar	١٥	– خمسة عشر
	- (Khamastāshar)		– (خمستاشر)
16	- Sittata 'ashar	١٦	– ستة عشر
	- (Sittāshar)		– (ستاشر)
17	- Sab'at 'ashar	١٧	– سبعة عشر
	- (Sab'atāshar)		– (سبعتاشر)
18	- Thamāniyat 'ashar	١٨	– ثمانية عشر
	- (Tamantāshar)		– (ثمنتاشر)
19	- Tis'at ashar	١٩	– تسعة عشر
	- (Tis'atāshar)	٠	– (تسعتاشر)
20	- 'Ishroon	٢٠	– عشرون
	- 'Ishrein		– عشرين
21	-Wā'Hid wa 'ishroon	٢١	– واحد وعشرون

22	- Ithnān wa 'ishroon	٢٢	اثنان وعشرون
30	Thalāthoon	٣٠	ثلاثون
40	Arb'aoon	٤٠	أربعون
50	Khamsoon	٥٠	خمسون
60	Sittoon	٦٠	ستون
70	Sab'oon	٧٠	سبعون
80	Thamānoon	٨٠	ثمانون
90	Tis'oon	٩٠	تسعون
100	- Mea'h - Miyyah	١٠٠	مائة (ميه)
101	- Mea'h wa wā'Hid - Miyyah wa wā'Hid	١٠١	مائة و واحد (ميه و واحد)
102	- Mea'h wa ithnān - Miyyah wa itnein	١٠٢	مائة واثنان (ميه واتنين)
200	Mea'tān	٢٠٠	مائتان

300	Thalāthu mea'h	٣٠٠	ثلاثمائة
400	Arba'u mea'h	٤٠٠	أربعمائة
500	Khamsu mea'h	٥٠٠	خمسمائة
600	Sittu mea'h	٦٠٠	ستمائة
700	Sab'u mea'h	٧٠٠	سبعمائة
800	Thamānu mea'h	٨٠٠	ثمانمائة
900	Tis'u mea'h	٩٠٠	تسعمائة
1000	Alf	١٠٠٠	ألف
1001	Alf wa wā'Hid	١٠٠١	ألف و واحد
1002	Alf wa ithnān	١٠٠٢	ألف و اثنان
2000	Alfān	٢٠٠٠	ألفان
3000	Thalāthatu alāf	٣٠٠٠	ثلاثة آلاف
4000	Arb'atu alāf	٤٠٠٠	أربعة آلاف
1000000	Milyoon	١٠٠٠٠٠٠	مليون

133

Other books (in Arabic) for the Writer

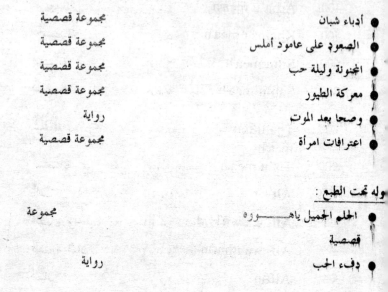

مجموعة قصصية — أدباء شبان

مجموعة قصصية — الصعود على عامود أملس

مجموعة قصصية — المجنونة وليلة حب

مجموعة قصصية — معركة الطيور

رواية — وصحا بعد الموت

مجموعة قصصية — اعترافات امرأة

وله تحت الطبع :

مجموعة — الحلم الجميل ياهـــــزوزه قصصية

رواية — دفء الحب

Part II (Egyptian Arabic)

All these books are available in Dar al-Ma'rif bookshop
Writer's phone : 5623318 & 3936123